CHATTO & WINDUS

*A Brief Account of the Firm's Origin,
History and Development*

CHATTO & WINDUS

*A Brief Account of the Firm's Origin,
History and Development*

BY

OLIVER WARNER

updated by

P. J. TURNER
and others

Chatto & Windus
LONDON

Published in 1991 by
Chatto & Windus Ltd
20 Vauxhall Bridge Road
London SW1V 2SA

A CIP catalogue record for this book is available from the
British Library

ISBN 0 7011 1963 2

Phototypeset by Intype, London

Printed and bound in Great Britain
Mackays of Chatham PLC
Chatham, Kent

I

IN 1955, the year when the firm of Chatto & Windus celebrated its centenary, the occasion was marked by a gay and informal evening party. This was held on 6 July at 23 Knightsbridge, and authors, fellow publishers and others, eminent and less eminent, met and enjoyed themselves. A few of them may even have heard the brief and characteristic speech made by Ian Parsons from a table top. It was one of welcome: there were no boasts.

There was also a more permanent memorial. This took the form of a substantial book. It was printed at the Oxford University Press and was called *A Century of Writers, 1855–1955*. It consisted of well over 700 pages and had 21 illustrations, some of them hitherto unpublished. The bulk of the work consisted of an anthology drawn from items which had carried the Chatto & Windus imprint. The selection was edited by D. M. Low, who died in 1972. He was a very old friend of the firm, and the biographer of Gibbon. Preceding the anthology there was a short history of the firm, which is the basis of the present work.

It is now a good many years since *A Century of Writers* appeared. As there is a continuing demand not only from people who join the firm, but from a wider public, for an accessible account of how Chatto & Windus came into being and how its history has evolved, opportunity has been taken to enlarge the original material and to bring it up to date.

Much has happened in the intervening decades, but nothing tragic except, alas, for the passing of men and women whose work was published by Chatto & Windus or who helped in its administration. On the other hand, there have been developments, all of which have brought prob-

1

lems and excitements, and a necessary and continuing infusion of new blood has not been lacking.

Incidentally, the centenary was not the only occasion of celebratory work. In 1926 the firm published a *Chatto and Windus Almanack* with illustrations by Albert Rutheston and contributions from some of the writers who at that time graced the list. A second *Almanack*, this time without original writing but with designs by Stanley Spencer, appeared in 1927; and there was an illustrated *Chatto and Windus Miscellany* in 1928 which has become a collector's piece, since it contained material some of which has not appeared elsewhere.

II

For a century the imprint 'Chatto & Windus' has been associated with varying kinds of books, and for many years longer, ever since the foundation of the business by John Camden Hotten, the firm has had vigorous direction. Although the value of the Hotten and, later, of the Chatto & Windus trade-mark has altered over the decades, the firm's name has seldom been placed on writing which, at the time of publication, did not appear to be good of its kind. Much has stood the test of years; some proportion may have survival quality as long as English is read.

Any sketch of the history of the business itself will be, from the very nature of publishing, largely one of personalities, for the good publisher habitually exercises individual taste and judgement. It may therefore be appropriate to consider the more vivid figures of the past, and some of the changes in emphasis in the products of the firm.

Chatto & Windus are not the only London publishers whose founder has been thought worthy of inclusion in the *Dictionary of National Biography*, but the honour is sufficiently uncommon to be worth pondering. Hotten was a remarkable and in some respects a puzzling character, but he built to endure, and it is probable that he knew it. He never did anything without purpose, and he had skill in creating lasting values, in a sphere which has always demanded acumen. A firm which can span a century and more and remain as vital as it was in its childhood, with its imprint respected today as much as at any time in the past, will in fact have been guided by a succession of astute people. Astute—and stable: for it is an impressive fact that during the ninety-eight years in which the firm was a private partnership, there were only five successive senior partners. And in every single instance, apart from Hotten himself, these heads of the firm took their place after much experience with their predecessors.

The founder, John Camden Hotten, was born in 1832, in the reign of William IV. He lived to be only forty-three, yet he crowded much into his brief life. Both his parents were Cornish: perhaps his fire and energy were Celtic: but he was brought up as a Londoner, at Clerkenwell, where his father had become established as a master-carpenter. At fourteen he was apprenticed to John Petheram, a bookseller of Chancery Lane, and soon discovered his vocation. A contributor to *Notes and Queries* once estimated that Hotten had a hand, often the sole hand, in no fewer than twenty-five books, mainly, though not exclusively, of an antiquarian sort, and the full list may never now be agreed.

He used pseudonyms, including the singular one of Titus A. Brick, and his gifts to the world included a *Slang Dictionary*. His most ambitious work, which a modern collector described as being, in his opinion, 'next to Lowndes's *Bibliographers' Manual*, probably the largest work of labour of its kind performed by one man during the last century', was an annotated catalogue of 20,000 books relating to the Topography and Family History of England and Wales. Like almost everything Hotten put a hand to, it is still worth consulting.

Hotten's interests were diverse, and he was very percipient. For instance he must have been among the first to realise the appeal of philately, for in 1864 he published at a shilling Bellars and Davie's *Standard Guide to Postage Stamp Collecting*. When in due time he came to publish in a large way, his list included not only a fine edition of *The Book of Common Prayer*, but a history of flogging! There were *Songs of the Nativity* and, to balance, a *History of Playing Cards*, with coloured illustrations: and there was a *Modern Confectioner*, written from data supplied by William Jeanes, chief confectioner at Messrs. Gunter's, then of Berkeley Square. The summit of elegance in production, in which Hotten took some pride, was reached in 1869: in that year he issued a version of Alban Butler's *Lives of the Saints*. It cost £7, 'enriched with fifty-one exquisite Full-page Miniatures, in gold silk velvet, preserved in a case', to quote the special announcement.

While still in his teens, Hotten went with his brother to America. The fruits of this visit became apparent soon after 1855, when he set up his business, first as bookseller, then as bookseller and publisher, at 151*b* Piccadilly, which surviving photographs show as a two-storied Georgian building, in brick. The premises have long disappeared, in favour of the Ritz Hotel. Though small, Hotten's enterprise prospered: his 'literary knowledge and shrewd intelligence collected around him a large circle of acquaintances', says the *Dictionary of National Biography*. In those few words are expressed much of the secret of successful book trafficking: and they refer to a time when Piccadilly was a centre for the book trade to a far greater extent than it has since been.

Hotten began his business in the year that the well-known publisher, William Pickering, also of Piccadilly, was gathered to his fathers, and it is significant that Hotten's

4

earliest trade-list contains many items bearing the beautiful anchor and dolphin design of Pickering's Aldine Edition of the poets. Other catalogues followed in quick succession, including an extensive offer of Tracts, Manuscripts, and Pamphlets, and a selection from the libraries of Samuel Rogers, the banker-poet, and of Lord Alvanley. Hotten had a shrewd touch, where books were concerned. All he did bears signs of that. By the end of the fifties he was busily introducing American work to English readers. In time his list came to include Mark Twain, Bret Harte, Artemus Ward, Oliver Wendell Holmes, C. G. Leland, J. R. Lowell, Edgar Allan Poe, Walt Whitman, Ambrose Bierce, and others important in the history of American letters.

Alas, Hotten's rôle in the reciprocal literary traffic between the United States and this country was not altruistic. Although a long line of illustrious English writers, Dickens among them, suffered from piracy of their work in the United States, and complained of it in no meek terms, yet the founder of the firm of Chatto & Windus, along with others, did his best to see that the business was not all one way. In his time, very few Americans took such steps as they could, or were necessary, to copyright their work in this country, and they suffered much. Where Hotten had the advantage over his confrères was that he knew the American field better than they did, and made unscrupulous use of that knowledge. These are strong words, but evidence of their truth is contained in an important though forgotten letter which Mark Twain published in *The Spectator* for 20 September 1872. This was a sally against Hotten, who, though within the law, had apparently published the writer's books without paying him a penny. That was not all!

My books are bad enough [said Mark Twain] just as they are written; then what must they be after Mr. John Camden Hotten has composed half a dozen chapters and added the same to them? Sometimes, when I read one of these additional chapters constructed by Mr. John Camden Hotten, I feel as if I wanted to take a broom-stick and go and knock that man's brains out. Not in anger, for I feel none. Oh! not in anger! but only to see, that is all. Mere idle curiosity.

Apparently one of Hotten's beliefs was that 'Carl Byng' was, like 'Mark Twain', a pseudonym for Samuel Clemens. If so, he was wrong. Mark Twain said so, adding:

How would this sinful aborigine feel if I were to call him John Camden Hottentot? I do honestly believe it would throw him into a brain fever, if there was not an insuperable obstacle in the way.

Mark Twain ended by saying that the firm of George Routledge were the only British publishers who paid him for his work. It should be added that when Andrew Chatto took on Hotten's business, the year after the letter appeared, relations with Mark Twain were established on the happiest basis, and remained so ever afterwards.

III

In 1866 various landmarks stood out in Hotten's business life. He published his beautiful Chiswick Press edition of the Prayer Book. He also issued a *History of Signboards*, which was in regular demand for many years, and which has been reprinted. This book is interesting for many reasons. The title-page states that it was written by Jacob Larwood and John Camden Hotten, and the dedication is to Thomas Wright, the author of a *Caricature History of the Georges* which, with its colour plates and its large and small editions, was long popular on Hotten's list. Larwood was the pseudonym of a Dutchman, Herman Diederik Johan van Schevichaven, who numbered among his gifts an ability in simple line drawing. Many of his illustrations enliven the

6

pages. One more notable fact about this book is that it appears to have been printed by (not *for*) the publisher. As the same notice occurs in one or two others of the Hotten series, it is probable that he combined a printing press with his other activities.

Another event in this memorable year was the publication of *Poems and Ballads* by Algernon Charles Swinburne. The event demands more than passing reference, since it permanently affected the nature of Hotten's business. Hitherto he had been known mainly as a specialist in certain lines—Americana, books with an antiquarian flavour, and what might be called historical oddities. Now, entirely of his own volition, he became publisher to a young creative artist of genius. He had ceased to be merely the 'astute purveyor', in the cold phrase of Swinburne's biographer, Sir Edmund Gosse, with a 'somewhat dingy imprint'. He had transformed himself into what every publisher must become if he wishes his name to mean anything in literary history—a vital collaborator, willing to finance and to market wares which possess inspiring, experimental, and even explosive qualities.

The issue of *Poems and Ballads* was in fact the most important single event since the foundation of the firm, and it may well have appeared so at the time. It took courage, and this was, in the long run, thoroughly rewarded. Meanwhile Hotten experienced the difficulties as well as the excitements of issuing the work of a man who possessed, pre-eminently, the artistic temperament.

The detailed circumstances of the first transaction were as follows. Swinburne, who was then just under thirty with a reputation gained through his poetic plays and through *Atalanta in Calydon*, which had appeared in 1865, had sent *Poems and Ballads* to the firm of Moxon, who had published his earlier work. Moxon himself was dead, but the sage advice once given him by Wordsworth was remembered by his successor, Bertrand Payne: 'first acquire a competence, then practise virtue'. Payne had already sent advance copies of *Poems and Ballads* to the newspapers for review, when he suddenly began to hear whispers. They grew. *The Saturday Review* was known to be ready to print a fierce attack on the morals of the poet. Worse still, *The Times* was said to be preparing a broadside which would include a demand for the criminal prosecution of the publisher.

Payne was horrified. On 5 August 1866 he withdrew the book from sale, 'without consulting me, without warning, and without compensation', in Swinburne's words: 'a victim of sudden and craven panic' in those of Gosse.

It was at this point that Hotten stepped in. He paid £200 for the existing copies of *Poems and Ballads*, acquiring also the sheets of Swinburne's essay on Blake, which appeared two years later 'with facsimile Paintings, coloured by hand', and also his earlier work. In fact, he took over the poet as a going concern.

The success of *Poems and Ballads* was immediate, though it had violent denunciators, and not long after publication Swinburne wrote to Sir Richard Burton, of the *Arabian Nights*, to say that 'one anonymous letter from Dublin threatened me, if I did not suppress my book within six weeks from that date, with castration'.

By 1869 *Poems and Ballads* was advertised as being in its third edition, though Swinburne's bibliographer, the late T. J. Wise, went so far as to say: 'I have been forced to the conclusion that Hotten repeatedly reprinted *Poems and Ballads* without any notification of the fact appearing upon the title-page.' He found it 'impossible to imagine that one single edition, following the first (which consisted of 1,000 copies only) would have sufficed to meet the circulation that undoubtedly existed'. Hotten, at any rate, was pushing Swinburne in no half-hearted way.

It would be pleasant to record that the relationship, begun with such enterprise, thenceforward blossomed. Alas, it was not so. From the outset it was uneasy. Swinburne chafed in Hotten's care, and as early as 1871 he had *Songs Before Sunrise* published elsewhere. Hotten was so angry that he threatened legal action, but the matter was temporarily smoothed, and the book was taken over three years later by Chatto & Windus. In fact Swinburne's relations with the firm (though never with Hotten personally) in the end became easier. When the poet came under the care of Watts-Dunton at The Pines, Putney, in his later years, he allowed his mentor to transact all his business for him, except that with Hotten's pupil and successor, Andrew Chatto.

A very careful study of the Swinburne-Hotten relationship has been made by an American scholar, John S. Mayfield, who, after the appearance of *A Century of Writers*, gave it as his opinion that Hotten:

must have been a prodigy of some sort, and he must have possessed an unlimited amount of energy. He was, I believe, a bit bewildered in his Swinburne relationship. There were so many people dealing with him *for* the poet, and 'on order' from the poet. That Hotten could never produce any written agreement he had with Swinburne regarding the publication of *Poems and Ballads* appears to stem from this condition, plus the fact that Hotten was inclined to believe and to trust those who dealt in the name of the poet.

In the end Hotten was wronged, I believe, by Swinburne suddenly taking his work elsewhere without notice, but at the same time Hotten profited above and beyond what he reported to Swinburne.

Of one thing I am certain: Hotten saved Swinburne's literary life by courageously issuing *Poems and Ballads* following its suppression by the firm Moxon, and Hotten was the only publisher in London who would undertake the project.

For seven years after his dramatic appropriation of Swinburne, Hotten continued to prosper, and to build up his list. The episode seems to have imbued him with even more vigour than before, and he flourished in strength right up

9

to the time of his death, on 14 June 1873. He was then living at Maitland Park Villas, Haverstock Hill, Hampstead.

There is now no exact means of telling what manner of man Hotten was. His creativity is indisputable. It was amusingly alluded to by D. M. Low, when the firm was preparing the centenary anthology. Low suggested that there might be worse titles for the book than 'Hotten and his Little Tots'.

Hotten's boldness was shown first in his setting up so early in life in the heart of the West End, then by his sustained success, and finally in the matter of Swinburne. There were stories long current of authors, in search of their due, seeking him out at his private address, to be met with a dusty answer; but the fact remains that when he died, at an age when many men are only just beginning to find themselves, he had built up a sturdy business which showed every sign that it would last.

Nearly thirty years after Hotten's death, *The Daily News*, in the issue of 27 July 1901, announced that 'an Indianapolis literary Society are about to place a tablet to J. C. Hotten, the famous Piccadilly publisher, in their library, as an acknowledgement of his services in introducing certain famous American authors to the British reading public'. No irony was intended: and it is true that even today Hotten's own books, and many that bear his imprint, are sought for and cherished.

IV

During his eighteen years' reign Hotten had moved from No. 151*b* to Nos. 74 and 75 Piccadilly, premises nearly opposite the first site. His successor, Andrew Chatto, who had been with the firm since the age of fifteen, had a literary background. His father, William Andrew Chatto, was a versatile writer, author of a standard work on wood-engraving which was reissued, in due time, as an act of filial piety. When Hotten died, Andrew Chatto bought the business from the widow for £25,000. He was joined in not very active partnership by W. E. Windus, who wrote narrative and lyric verses. Windus's first book, *Under Dead Leaves*, was published by Hotten in 1871, and his second, *Broadstone Hall and Other Poems*, appeared with his own name and that of Chatto on the title-page. It is as well to add that the last of the three volumes recorded as from him in the catalogue of the British Museum, *Elizabeth Stuart* (a dramatic sketch), was issued by the firm of Gubbins in the Isle of Wight—perhaps a pointer to publishers not to risk their more recondite verse on their own list.

W. E. Windus is sometimes confused with W. L. Windus, an historical painter who exhibited in the forties and fifties of the last century. W. E. is now scarcely quotable, though his appreciation of the good things of life may be illustrated by an unexpected Bacchanalian from *Broadstone Hall*:

> Come fill another bumper, lad,
>   The wine is old and mellow,
> The toast I'll give shall not be sad—
>   'Here's to our friends', old fellow!
>
> For life's too short to fret and pine,
>   Or brood too much in sorrow;
> Our foes we'll drown in generous wine,
>   And leave them till tomorrow.

At the end of Windus's book of verse was a catalogue, forty pages long, still full of Hotteniana. The date was 1875, and it was in fact the second or third issued by the newly named firm. The first which is now in the archives, dated July 1874, had as its principal item Maclise's *Gallery of Illustrious Literary Characters*, a demy quarto of over 400 pages. It was priced at 31s. 6d. in cloth, 'or in morocco elegant,

11

70/-'. There followed announcements of Cruikshank's *Comic Almanack*, Poems by Charles and Mary Lamb, Mayhew's *London Characters*, Theodore Hook's *Humorous Works*, Swinburne's *Bothwell: a Tragedy*, and a large assortment of American items.

In the year 1876 Percy Spalding brought a breeze into the business. Spalding, who is still affectionately remembered by older people, particularly for his constant ejaculation, which sounded like 'Nce', was the son of H. B. Spalding, of the firm of Spalding and Hodge, well known as paper merchants. Four years after his arrival the partnership moved to 214 Piccadilly, a few yards from the Circus, where it continued for nineteen years. It has been settled since 1898 in the neighbourhood of St. Martin's Lane, first at No. 111, then after 1918 at Nos. 97 and 99, and finally, until the late 1980s, just round the Coliseum corner at 40 and 42 William IV Street. The move to 214 Piccadilly coincides very roughly with the change-over from bookselling and publishing to publishing pure and simple.

If Windus, as a man of business, remains shadowy, there is charming evidence about both Andrew Chatto and Percy Spalding. These two men, between them, could have claimed credit for establishing the firm not merely on a respectable but an assured basis.

Chatto was his own reader. He was a man of wide interests, an amateur scientist and astronomer, a 'cellist and a yachtsman. Mr. Swinnerton recalls him in *The Bookman's London* as:

a gentle elderly man with a rolling walk, genially sweet in manner to every member of his staff, and much loved.

Almost better loved still was his partner, Percy Spalding, who did not pretend to any literary taste, but put his hands in his pockets, jingled his keys and coppers, whistled *Meet Me To-Night in Dreamland* and said to all authors, whatever their pretensions, 'Nce, give us a rattling good story!'

12

Another account of Andrew Chatto senior was given by George Frommholz, for long production manager of the firm. He remembers him as looking, what indeed he must have been,

a typical English gentleman. Rather under average height, heavily built, bearded, and with pince-nez. He, with Mr. Spalding sitting opposite to him at the huge desk they used to occupy, simply oozed confidence. I don't wonder they published for so many eminent authors.

Mr. Chatto himself always went to Smith's and Mudie's for subscription orders for new books. This duty was never delegated to the travellers. The same hansom cabby drove him to and fro.

Chatto's two sons followed him into the literary line. Tom, the younger, joined the well-known antiquarian firm of Pickering and Chatto; the elder, Andrew, was at least a nominal partner of his father from 1893 onwards to 1919, though his real interests were out-doors.

It was in fact the elder Chatto and Percy Spalding who guided the long and prosperous middle era of the firm. In the year that Spalding became a partner, much of the stock and copyright formerly belonging to Henry George Bohn was acquired in consideration of £20,000 and from the seventies to the early years of the present century the firm was eminent both as general and as fiction publishers. The list in due time came to include the works of Sir Walter Besant, Wilkie Collins, Justin McCarthy, Ouida, Charles Reade, R. L. Stevenson, and many others important in their era. It also included at least one or two books by others of the more notable writers of the later Victorian and the Edwardian age, including Hardy's *Under the Greenwood Tree* and some vintage Trollope. Moreover, the firm won the good-will both of the trade and of its writers. Besant, the first President of the Society of Authors, once remarked: 'I should like to see my friend Chatto driving in a gilded coach!'; while perhaps the best-known tribute ever paid to the concern came in the form of a letter to Andrew Chatto from R. L. Stevenson, sent from Bournemouth on 3 October 1884:

If you don't know that you have a good author [wrote Stevenson] I know that I have a good publisher. Your fair, open and handsome dealings are a good point in my life, and do more for my crazy health than has yet been done by any doctor.

This letter was written two years after the publication by Cassell of *Treasure Island*, a book which first brought Stevenson fame, and one which has been a big seller ever since. Tradition long maintained that Andrew Chatto lost this jewel through suggesting to Stevenson that he should set aside an earlier effort in fiction which he had proposed for publication. The facts do not support this. Stevenson wrote *Treasure Island* as a serial for *Young Folks*, and was delighted when he was offered £100 for it by Cassell. But the result of his success was that his father bought back R.L.S.'s earlier copyrights and transferred the stocks to Chatto & Windus. Although the firm did not, indeed, publish all Stevenson's later books, the association was long, close and profitable. Chatto crowned his services in a way which touched the author's heart. In 1890 Stevenson wrote, in white-hot passion, a defence of the memory of Father Damien of the Molokai leper colony, whose good name had been assailed in Australia by a Presbyterian parson of the name of Hyde. It was a splendid piece of prose and the invective demolished his victim. Stevenson presented the pamphlet to Chatto, refusing all payment, saying that 'he was not a cannibal, and could not eat the flesh of Dr. Hyde'. Chatto, not to be outdone in generosity, sent the author's share of the profits to Molokai.

V

It was D. H. Lawrence who, in an apt phrase, once spoke of the Victorian heads of the firm as 'old-flavoured folk'. They conducted a large business without aid of telephone or typewriter. They made outright agreements on half sheets of notepaper, and they tended to view office routine almost as an extension of home. In winter time, the building was warmed by open coal fires. In summer, Percy Spalding regularly rode on horse-back in the Park during what would now be termed 'office hours'. There is much to be said for such a felicitous way of life, but publishing has always been a competitive activity, and from time to time strong injections of new people, ideas, and capital become necessary. It was so with Chatto & Windus.

Seeking vigour, the firm imported a whirlwind in the person of Philip Lee-Warner. He arrived in 1905.

A long whisking figure [Mr. Swinnerton recalls], his eyes always blinking, and little tufts of cotton wool dotting his face where he had cut his skin while shaving. He curved as he whisked, and he had a sweet grin. Really brilliant, but a gambler. . . . He sniffed his speeches: 'Look here, P. Sp*o*lding . . .' He always called Spalding Sp*o*lding.

He was liked by everybody, and the memory long lingered in the office of how he would dictate his letters lying on the floor with a cushion at the back of his head. So startling were Lee-Warner's projects that, within three years, he had shaken the partnership to its roots, and brought it within sight of disaster. The horrid vision receded: so did the dazzling newcomer, who continued onwards in his zestful career to found the Medici Society. One of his memorials is the head of Minerva which appeared in a catalogue of 1908 and which has since been used on the firm's envelopes.

15

Lee-Warner left a varied legacy. His interest in art had led him to acquire excellent but expensive books on that subject. He made use of the services of that great scholar, Sir Israel Gollancz, as general editor of the 'King's Classics' and the 'Medieval Library'. He set standards in book production—exemplified in the fine Florence Press editions, the type specially designed for the series by Herbert P. Horne—which have been maintained ever since; and he introduced into the firm two young men, Geoffrey Whitworth and Frank Swinnerton, who served it for twenty years apiece, brought in many new authors, and gained renown later in other fields, Whitworth as founder of the British Drama League, Swinnerton as novelist, critic, broadcaster, and author of a highly individual work on a subject of which he knew much: *The Georgian Literary Scene*.

Andrew Chatto senior did not long survive Lee-Warner's departure. He retired in 1911 and died two years later. He was the strongest link with the past, but there was no abrupt break with tradition, for after he had gone affairs were conducted by Percy Spalding and, less enthusiastically, by the younger Chatto. Early in 1914 Charles Prentice arrived from Oxford, but he had little time to become familiar with the problems of publishing before being caught up into the military machine and finding himself in line of battle in Flanders.

Of the days of the earlier St. Martin's Lane premises, when the firm was in the magazine as well as the book-publishing field, Frommholz wrote:

Looking back, it seems to me that authors, budding and otherwise, would float in and out almost at will. I think the most frequent visitor was George R. Sims, who seemed to make a habit of arriving just as the partners were going upstairs for lunch. In those days the firm employed a man and wife as caretakers, and the caretaker's wife always prepared lunch, which was taken on the second floor. Those were the days!—and if old Jack Smith the housekeeper was caught napping when George R. Sims bowled in, he could always run out for a steak or a dozen oysters and a pint of stout.

George R. Sims is almost forgotten, but his prodigious output included the verses 'It Was Christmas Day in the Workhouse' (assuredly not based on his experience in St. Martin's Lane), and he paid his old friend Andrew Chatto a left-handed compliment in calling his hair-restorer Tatcho, which was an anagram of his name.

It was chiefly in his capacity as a journalist that Sims grew familiar to the firm, though they also published his novels. Chatto & Windus were then prominent in the field of magazine publishing. For many years they handled the old-established *Gentleman's Magazine*, which survived, with breaks, from 1731 to 1922; the *Belgravia*, in which Hardy's *The Return of the Native* first appeared and to which Ouida contributed, which was extant from 1866 to 1899; and the *Idler*, associated with Jerome K. Jerome, which ran from 1892 to 1911. Geoffrey Whitworth's bi-monthly *Drama* had a year's run, from July 1919 to July 1920, in the firm's catalogue, after which there came a break with the tradition of journal publishing, which was revived in the thirties.

The older way of life must have had good moments. For instance, there was period when profusely illustrated catalogues came annually from the great London stores. One applicant from the Gold Coast, who perhaps looked to Chatto & Windus to produce a similar type of article, wrote as follows:

Dear Sirs; I have the honour to inform you. Please send me your books, and you have the greatest honour. O death, where is thy sting! Yours etc.

A final recollection by Frommholz from the pre–1914 years concerns a sporting event, comparatively rare in the firm's annals owing to its modest size. A challenge to a football

17

match was offered: it came from either Messrs. Heinemann or Messrs. James Burn, the binders.

Jerseys were bought for the occasion, and in due course the team turned out in full regalia at Wormholt Farm, Shepherd's Bush. Mr. Swinnerton was in the side, but despite his and everybody else's efforts we were beaten by a large margin. Nobody appeared anxious to referee the game, but the situation was saved by an under-sized little fellow, a proper Cockney, coming up and asking us if he could officiate. He was a rough diamond, but he controlled the game well, and when it was over both sides made a collection for him. I don't know what the other team collected, but it must have been a much smaller amount than ours, for when we handed him the three or four shillings we had subscribed he looked at it, spat on the silver and said, 'Gawd, if I'd only known!'

Frommholz was himself one of those endearing people with an original sense of humour. Behind his desk in St. Martin's Lane he had a sliding panel in the wall which enabled him to pass material to the Reader in the next room without the need for walking down the passage. One day, handing through a bundle of heavily revised proofs, such as were not uncommon when printing was less expensive than it now is, he remarked: 'When I die, I hope some one will put on my tomb-stone: "Here lies Frommholz—sent up for a last Revise!"' '

VI

In the history of businesses there is sometimes a point, shortly after a major change of direction has taken place, when both past and future seem to be illuminated. In the instance of Chatto & Windus it could be said to have been reached in 1926. The past lingered. Percy Spalding still hung his glossy top-hat in the partner's cloak-room, though it was the last year in which he did so. The present was strong in personalities; something of the future could be discerned. Fresh standards were apparent; policy was forward looking. In that year the present writer, as a very young man, was somewhat dazzled at the offer to succeed Frank Swinnerton as reader. This post he held with great enjoyment for the next fourteen years until summoned away by the admiralty.

The guiding spirits of the twenties were Charles Prentice and Harold Raymond. Ian Parsons, who was to succeed Prentice as typographer, was even then editing the *Cambridge Review*, and in 1928 took Geoffrey Whitworth's place as art editor. Among the executives were a few who had been engaged by the historic Andrew Chatto; others were but recently from school. Evidences of Lee-Warner's three electric years as partner could still be seen on the walls in the shape of coloured prints.

Spalding's successor as senior partner, Charles Prentice, was a remarkable man. One of the neatest attempts to describe him was made by Mr. John Fothergill of *An Inkeeper's Diary*. He called him 'a genius in eiderdown clothing'. Probably no publisher ever had more books dedicated to him than Prentice. Like many Scots, he was generous in the extreme, though like every man of sense he hated waste.

Prentice had an air of Mr. Pickwick, who was in fact one of his favourite characters in fiction. There was, however, a sharp difference. Prentice was shrewd; he had no illusions about life in general—he felt, like Conrad's Winnie Verloc, that it didn't bear looking into; he was a scholar; and both in literary matters and in book design he had wonderful taste. That is to say much. Proof resides in the firm's catalogues during the years in which he was most active— from 1919 to 1934. In proportion to its yearly output, Chatto & Windus maintained what was possibly the most distinguished list in London, both in content and in appearance. Lest this seems to be hyperbole, the words of a typographer of wide reputation may be called in evidence.

Chatto and Windus [wrote Mr. Ruari Mclean in *Modern Book Design*] have probably the longest unbroken record of excellence in book design of any London publishers still in business. They were good before 1900 . . . after the 1914 war, Chatto and Windus books were designed by Charles Prentice. Typical and familiar examples of his work are the first editions of C. E. Montague, R. H. Mottram, and Aldous Huxley. They have a quiet and unpretentious excellence; and like all well-made books they feel just right in the hand even before they are opened—a combination of size, thickness, weight of paper and the texture of the binding cloth.

'Quiet and unpretentious excellence' helps to describe Prentice, a man of silences. It was due to Harold Raymond that his discriminating books were more than collectors' pieces, were in fact merchandise widely distributed throughout the literate world.

Prentice and Raymond were heirs to an accumulation of fiction and miscellaneous works which had been swelling the catalogue for a great number of years. Grant Allen, Frank Barrett, Sir Hall Caine, B. M. Crocker, Dick Donovan with his detective stories, Manville Fenn, Florence Marryat, D. Christie Murray, James Payn, these are a random choice of names from lists in the decline of the Andrew Chatto era. One of Raymond's earliest problems, which he described in the Dent Memorial Lecture for 1938, was 'to job off an accumulation of works which had long ceased to sell. Those who regard Penguins as a modern portent may be surprised to hear that I found a stock of over three-quarters of a million sixpenny paper-covered works lying dormant on Chatto's shelves.' Upwards of eighty titles were concerned, and, as Raymond said: 'it was a *very* long fiction list that could produce that number of works which would pay to be re-set and sold at sixpence.'

20

If the past lay dormant on shelves, future sunlight was promised with the publication of Lytton Strachey's *Eminent Victorians* (1918) followed by *Queen Victoria* (1921). The effect of these books was considerable, and lasting. Strachey was a prominent member of the Bloomsbury Group, among whom were E. M. Forster, J. M. Keynes, Virginia and Leonard Woolf, G. E. Moore, Duncan Grant, Roger Fry, Clive Bell, and G. Lowes Dickinson. Many of them were associated either with Chatto & Windus or the Hogarth Press.

'Keynes and Strachey did not want to bring down the Victorian house', says Mr. J. K. Johnstone, the historian of the group, 'they wanted to sweep out some trash, move in some new furniture and re-arrange the rooms.' It was precisely this revivifying effort which Strachey achieved, not only on the outlook of his time but on the list of the firm with whom he chose to publish. His spirit was infectious. That they were ready to seize the opportunity offered by such writers as Strachey to revitalize the list is a measure of the skill of the new partners.

Prentice, having seen the firm increase in stature, had himself no wish to die in harness, and he was fortunate enough to have no reason for so doing. He ended his twenty years of partnership in 1934 and travelled in Greece, which had long been his wish. Alas, illness pursued him. He recovered sufficiently to make a brief return during the earlier part of the Second World War, when Raymond was alone, and later still did some typographical work for Penguin Books. Indeed, in his later years he seemed so much more his earlier self that his death, while on a visit to East Africa in 1949, came as a very great shock to those who knew him best.

After Prentice had retired, John McDougall joined Harold Raymond and Ian Parsons in a triumvirate which guided important events in the firm's history. The first was re-entry into the sphere of journal publishing. The second was the move to Chandos Street, the name of which was changed later to William IV Street.

It began with the publication of a review called *World*, edited by Vernon Bartlett, which, uniting later with *Review of Reviews*, was given new vigour as *World Review* at a time when foreign affairs were mounting towards the climax of European war. The paper at first appeared from the old premises at 97 and 99 St. Martin's Lane. Shortly after the move, which was made in 1935, came the successful launching of the *Geographical Magazine*, edited by Michael Huxley, which the firm published monthly for twenty-one years.

Less good fortune attended a lone but exciting excursion into weekly journalism. *Night and Day* ran—if 'raced' is not a more appropriate word— from July to December 1937, edited by John Marks, with Graham Greene as Literary Editor. It was a humorous paper of a kind which John Camden Hotten would surely have approved, since it had the poker-faced wit which is one of America's pleasures. Like a firework, *Night and Day* coruscated and went out. There are those who treasure their bound volumes, for it was years before anything remotely comparable was sponsored in this country. A large number of the leading writers and artists of today appeared in its columns during that rip-roaring half-year. Since the demise of *Night and Day* the firm has added other journals to its catalogue, *The Use of English*, an educational quarterly taken over in 1951, the *London Magazine*, which was published from William IV Street between 1954 and 1956, and the American *Partisan Review* which was marketed between 1963 and 1969.

Book publishing during the few years between the establishment of the new pattern of partnership and the outbreak of war became increasingly difficult. The general output of the trade continued to rise, without a corresponding response from the book-buying public. Times were hard, and war, which dispersed the personnel of the firm—Ian

Parsons went into the Royal Air Force and McDougall into the Admiralty—brought its own sharp problems. On the other hand it resolved others. The 'black-out', and shortage of alternative forms of entertainment, put a premium on reading at a time when the output of books had perforce been drastically curtailed. Trade gradually boomed. Towards the end of the war, almost any book could find a buyer. It had been so in the First World War. History was merely repeating itself. So were the inevitable shortages in materials, particularly paper.

Afterwards the partnership was re-formed. McDougall left to become head of a still older concern, Chapman & Hall Ltd. Mrs. Norah Smallwood, who had been in charge of design during the war years, became a partner in 1945. She was the proof of the fact that in publishing a secretary's desk may with time be exchanged for that of managing director, though only if the person concerned, in addition to exceptional ability, has resilience, energy, and taste.

In 1946 the firm took under its management the Hogarth Press, which had been founded at Richmond in 1917 by Leonard and Virginia Woolf. How this came about has been described by Leonard Woolf in the final volume of his auto-biography, *The Journey not the Arrival Matters* (1970). The crux of the matter was that he did not want to expand what for nearly thirty years had proved to be an individual, highly discriminating, successful and economically run venture. His business partner thought otherwise. In the upshot Leonard Woolf acquired sole possession. Part of the money to enable him to do this was supplied by Chatto & Windus. It was one of the smoothest transactions of its kind. Leonard Woolf recalls that the crisis arose from a letter received one breakfast time. 'When I had finished my kipper and coffee', he wrote, 'I had made up my mind on what I should do about the Hogarth Press. Before lunch I had succeeded in settling its future satisfactorily.' Just like that.

Leonard Woolf's stipulations that the Press 'should retain

its independence and not be absorbed in or controlled by Chatto, and that my general policy with regard to the kind of books which we had published, and with regard to expansion, would be maintained' was scrupulously observed. The Press later became a limited company, and Leonard Woolf remained on the board until his death in August 1969. He brought many distinguished books to the firm, quite apart from those of his wife and himself. There were the complete psychological works of Sigmund Freud, besides other key works on psychology and psycho-analysis. And at the time of the amalgamation or later, authors such as A. L. Barker, Laurie Lee, Henry Green, Christopher Isherwood, Edwin and Willa Muir, Jiri Mucha, William Plomer, Rainer Maria Rilke, William Sansom and Laurens van der Post had books in the Hogarth catalogue, which could claim to be among the most distinguished in London.

In 1953, when two years short of its centenary, Chatto & Windus ceased to be a private partnership, and became a limited company. At the time of the transformation, Harold Raymond was Chairman, and the board consisted of Ian Parsons, Norah Smallwood, Piers Raymond (Harold's son), who continued with the firm until he moved to Methuen in 1960, Peter Cochrane, who later joined the printing company of Butler & Tanner, with C. Day-Lewis as literary advisor. Day-Lewis later became a member of the board, and his appointment in 1968 as Poet Laureate not only reflected honour on the firm but emphasized the fact that poetry, at least since the days of Swinburne, had been one of its more important pre-occupations. Day-Lewis's death, in May 1972, brought sorrow far outside the firm to which he belonged. Among many tributes was one from Lord Butler, in his capacity as President of the Royal Society of Literature, who said: 'We shall miss him more than I can say, particularly because when we were in trouble or anxiety, we could always count on him for wise and sensible advice. He had a truly balanced character.' A fuller appreciation belongs elsewhere than in such a brief survey as this, but no one delighted in the Poet Laureate's personality more than those with whom he was brought into daily contact.

VII

There were those who, for sentimental reasons, were sad at the alteration of the firm's status, but it was in fact something of a feat to have survived as a private partnership for so long. 'Chatto & Windus Limited' retains the advantages of a private concern and has none of the forbidding aspects of commercial giants. It has not become impersonal, and it will be a shocking day if it ever does so.

Harold Raymond, who had seen the firm through so much vicissitude, including more than one narrow escape from the destruction of its premises during the Second World War, retired as Chairman in 1954. In the same year Peter Calvocoressi, whose wide experience and expert knowledge of international affairs added a valuable new dimension to the list, became a director. Two years later Raymond resigned from the board, to enjoy life in a particularly lovely part of Kent, and to travel, with his wife, even more strenuously than he had done in younger days. Calvocoressi was with the firm for twelve years before taking up a post at the University of Sussex. Geoffrey Trevelyan arrived in 1962 from de Havillands to take charge of educational and technical publishing. Three years later J. F. Charlton joined, after experience with Longmans, his special care being the more recondite works on the list of the Hogarth Press. In 1966 Hugo Brunner arrived from the Oxford University Press.

The gathering of the Hogarth Press within the Chatto & Windus fold had been a sign that the process of acquiring

25

other lists, which had begun as long ago as the 1870s, would be pursued as and when opportunity occurred. In 1954 Christopher's educational list, which dated back nearly half a century, was taken over, and in 1958 it was re-christened Chatto & Windus (Educational) Ltd. Ten years later, the children's list of the old-established Scots firm Oliver & Boyd was acquired, the books thereafter being published under the imprint 'Chatto Boyd & Oliver'. The firm was also, after 1969, associated with the Universities of St. Andrews and Dundee in publishing books under the imprint of the Scottish Academic Press, and after 1971, in partnership with the University of Sussex, those of Sussex University Press. The firm has also been responsible for publications of the Institute of Psychoanalysis and the International Institute for Strategic Studies.

Early in 1969 there occurred one of the greater events in the history of the concern. Ever since the Second World War, publishing houses with enviable lists had found it increasingly hard to resist take-overs or outright purchase on what might have seemed tempting terms. Chatto & Windus had side-stepped such persuasions, and so had Jonathan Cape. But the time came when the boards of both businesses felt that, in a world where everything seemed to be growing larger and larger at an ever-increasing pace, there was at least some safety in size. As their interests were the same and their standards comparable, what better course than to join forces?

The preliminaries took time. They had been briefly described by Michael Howard, son of G. Wren Howard, one of the founders of Jonathan Cape Ltd., widely regarded as the most outstanding general publishers to become established during the inter-war decades. The account appears in *Jonathan Cape, Publisher*, which appeared in 1971 to serve both as a history of the firm's first half-century and as a memorial of its chief personalities.

Ian Parsons announced the news in a confidential letter

to Chatto & Windus authors, thus ensuring that they were informed before the story 'broke' in the Press. He told them: 'We are about to join forces with Jonathan Cape. When I say "join forces" I mean just that.' A holding company would be formed, Chatto & Windus and Cape having an equal number of voting shares, and the right to appoint an equal number of directors to the board, of which Michael Howard and Ian Parsons would be joint chairmen.

'Our authors', the letter continued, 'will still be dealing with precisely the same people as before.' That was perhaps the most reassuring note, for some of the disturbances in the vital author–publisher relationship experienced after many amalgamations had to be endured to be believed.

'The advantages of this tie-up', the letter continued, 'are not solely or even mainly financial, though the resources of the combine will obviously be substantially larger than those which either party commands at present. The main point of the merger is to ensure, as far as this is humanly possible in these days, that we and Cape can continue to exist as independent concerns publishing the kind of books we have always published and responsible to nobody but ourselves and our authors.'

The letter concluded by remarking on the close personal and business friendships which had been enjoyed by members of the two firms for well over thirty years. It was to be marriage with mutual respect.

Reactions on the part of the authors were even more favourable than could have been hoped. One Chatto & Windus poet, Jennifer Couroucli, actually burst into song.

Chatto's is merging with Jonathan Cape—
Better to marry than burn,
Better to wed than to give in to rape
By a tempting Big Business concern.
For richer, not poorer, for better, not worse,
Till death do us part may you publish our verse.

27

This sentiment was echoed by William Plomer, who in a sprightly post-card wrote:

> Said Jonathan Cape,
> 'We've got a new shape.'
> 'Ship-shape,' said Chatto
> 'We're in the same bateau.'

VIII

As the fame of a publishing firm, to say nothing of its solvency, depends upon the writers for whom it markets, it is well to consider some of the works which have helped to give the imprint of Chatto & Windus its flavour. Time is the surest winnower, and it is interesting to note that those writings had survived, in the general catalogue, from Victorian and Edwardian days, right up to that period in the Second World War when so much good work became unobtainable, either through enemy action or material shortages.

Among general works, selections from Theodore Hook and Thomas Hood were still in print, together with some Richard Jefferies, George Macdonald, and Justin McCarthy, whose *History of Our Own Times* had once been a great money-spinner. There was still much Stevenson; W. N. P. Barbellion's *Journal of a Disappointed Man* was typical of the many fine books which were given continued life in the Phoenix Library, which Prentice had designed in 1927 to replace the earlier St. Martin's Library of pocket reprints. There were some specialist works; there were landmarks like Clive Bell's *Art*, F. R. Leavis's *New Bearings in English Poetry* and William Empson's *Seven Types of Ambiguity*; some Belloc and Chesterton; Arnold Bennett's plays; Sir W. S. Gilbert's comic operas; and some great translations— Constance Garnett's Chekhov and Gogol, C. K. Scott

Moncrieff's incomparable Proust and Stendhal, Vizetelly's Zola. And there were a few doughty old stand-bys like Dr. E. C. Brewer's *Reader's Handbook*, invaluable to puzzle addicts.

In fiction there was some more Arnold Bennett; there was Besant, both alone and in collaboration with James Rice; Wilkie Collins in force; Mrs. B. M. Croker in force; Bret Harte in force; Ouida likewise. Ouida was extravagant, and soon spent the large sums which according to current practice were paid outright for her novels. Then there were warning notes from Chatto or Spalding, and she curbed her pace for a while. There was Charles Reade in quantity; Mark Twain virtually *in toto*; there were juveniles perpetually in demand, prominent among them Helen Bannerman's *Little Black Sambo*, first published in 1899 and still going strong. There was that phenomenal best-seller of the early twenties, Daisy Ashford's *The Young Visiters*. There could indeed be no complaint that the firm's products did not last, and a number of books, such as F. L. Lucas's four-volume edition of the plays of John Webster and Leonard King's *History of Babylonia*, were evidence of that respect for scholarship without which no publisher of standing and reputation may be said to have done his whole duty.

Among contemporaneous books, Lytton Strachey's earlier biographies were the precursors of a succession of distinguished works, including a long and extremely varied list, begun in 1920 with *Leda* and *Limbo*, by Aldous Huxley, one of the small band of English writers with a truly international reputation. There were books by Julian Huxley, Roger Fry, David Garnett, J. B. S. Haldane, Norman Douglas, Richard Hughes and the Nobel Prize-winners Par Lagerkvist and William Faulkner, the latter an American novelist of striking originality whose appearance on the list would have gratified John Camden Hotten, as would that of Clarence Day, author of *Life with Father*. There were the earlier novels of Rosamond Lehmann; Wyndham Lewis's polemics; A. A. Milne's plays; C. E. Montague; the *Spanish Farm* series of R. H. Mottram; Wilfred Owen's war poems; the entire range of works of T. F. Powys; the novels, stories and poems of Sylvia Townsend Warner, whose first novel, *Lolly Willowes*, was one of the most graceful books that Prentice ever designed, and the work of V. S. Pritchett. Nor should the highly popular novels of Margaret Irwin and Ann Bridge be omitted.

More recent additions to the list include books of infinite variety by Sir Compton Mackenzie; scholarship and criticism by such authorities as Muriel Bradbrook, F. R. Leavis, E. M. W. Tillyard and Basil Willey; poetry; fiction, including a series of works by Iris Murdoch and Elizabeth Taylor, and a number of impressive war books such as F. Spencer Chapman's *The Jungle is Neutral*. Moreover, just as in the First World War the firm produced one of the pioneer books on air fighting, the letters of Harold Rosher, after the Second they published the narratives of outstanding pilots like 'Johnnie' Johnson and Pierre Clostermann, as well as those of more senior air force officers. Again, Sir David Bone, who was one of the rare men to occupy posts of high responsibility in both World Wars, added *Merchantman Rearmed* to his invaluable *Merchantman at Arms*, which derived from experience between 1914 and 1918. In general it may be said today, as of earlier periods, that in specialist studies such as archaeology, as well as in general books and fiction, the firm continues a long-established tradition. Series such as the Zodiac Press and the Landmark Library range of books have also helped to keep people in mind of works of lasting interest and importance. In fact there are few serious writers who have not either themselves contributed items to the list, or who do not owe stimulus to some who adorn it.

The firm is one of the few who are prepared to add poetry to their catalogue, fully aware that it is seldom remunerative except perhaps in the very long run, and not often then. The combined Chatto and Hogarth lists include volumes by a remarkable number of distinguished writers including Patric Dickinson, D. J. Enright, Jon Stallworthy, Laurie Lee, George Mackay Brown, Jon Silkin, Norman MacCaig and Terence Tiller. Incidentally, Laurie Lee is one of the poets who, in respect of another activity, has become a best-seller. His *Cider with Rosie* has rivalled Daisy Ashford's *The Young Visiters*, the runaway success of a much earlier vintage, in popular demand.

Many sided as the firm's activities have been, inter-trade obligations have also been included among them. It has actively supported every means by which the use of books could be increased. In this direction Harold Raymond will long be remembered for his origination of the Book Token Scheme. For many years this has proved itself to be one of the most successful and extensive co-operative efforts to further the sale of books, both among those who habitually frequent book-shops and those who, in the ordinary way, do not.

Raymond's example was followed by Ian Parsons, who served as President of the Publishers Association from 1957 to 1959 and was the first member of the firm to be elected to that office. Not unusually, his tenure of this important post involved him in a considerable amount of complicated trade negotiation. And shortly afterwards he was involved, as a witness, in the five-week-long defence of the Net Book Agreement, regarded as a sheet anchor of the trade by publishers and booksellers alike.

IX

If any general truths may be perceived through such a story as is outlined here, it is that good writers attract other good writers; that it is sound to develop along regular lines

31

of interest, whether fashionable or not; and that it rarely pays to lower standards in the hope of passing success.

Conditions in publishing remain difficult. Counter-attractions to reading become more and more pervasive. An active policy was never more necessary. But from the ever-fresh appearance of the seasonal lists an observer, however cautious, might surely be inclined to predict that the history of Chatto & Windus would extend indefinitely, that the high summer was by no means at an end. The accumulated harvest of pleasure, profit and variety already gathered into the catalogue is so rich that any annalist of the firm's activities is faced not with lack of material but with the need for selection: never a simple task. In a way, it is a fortunate situation, yet it is one which may daunt my successor when, in the fullness of time, he comes to survey the second century.

Whatever his problem may be, he is unlikely to be able to include a more generous tribute than one which came in 1949 from the Earl of Crawford and Balcarres, who was writing to thank the firm for one of its publications.

A member of the public has as a rule no opportunity of expressing his views of any publication except by buying or refusing to buy it: but you have given me a chance which I take of showing my appreciation of the consistently high level, the example you set to others, and the quality of content and production which has for so long characterized all the work of Chatto & Windus for so many years, and the pleasure and encouragement this has given to thousands besides myself.

CHATTO & WINDUS
1973–1991

BY

P. J. TURNER

and others

In 1973 Oliver Warner remarked that 'Conditions in publishing remain difficult . . .'; in 1991 as this updating goes to press they remain, if anything, more difficult than ever. Chatto & Windus has not survived untouched by the powerful pressures that have affected the industry over the past two decades. The firm has had to adapt to new technology and times of economic recession; despite this it has managed to build up its reputation as one of the leading literary publishing houses in London.

After Chatto's historic merger with Jonathan Cape in 1969, the two firms took their cooperation a stage further. Cape had been part owners of The Bodley Head until it was sold to Max Reinhardt in 1957. The Bodley Head had remained closely linked to Cape, and in August 1973 joined the Chatto-Cape publishing partnership. A new holding company was formed, of which Max Reinhardt became Joint-Chairman together with Graham C. Greene of Cape and Ian Parsons of Chatto. The three firms were thus able to pool their resources in marketing, warehousing, distribution and accountancy. Chatto at this time were still in William IV Street, Bodley Head in Bow Street, and the Cape offices were at 30 Bedford Square.

From the late 1960s and into the 1970s various decisions changed the nature and scope of the Chatto list. In 1972 Chatto sold its educational list to Hart-Davis Educational, now part of Harper Collins. In 1976 it ended its partnership (set up in 1969) with Scottish Academic Press, and likewise the association between Chatto and Sussex University Press was ended in 1977. Against a background of growing specialisation and the need for a sales force with specialist knowledge it was deemed sensible not to continue in these educational and academic markets but to concentrate on what Chatto was renowned for: general books and literature.

During this period the Chatto board consisted of six members, dominated by the long-standing partnership of Ian Parsons and Norah Smallwood: Hugo Brunner was appointed to the Chatto board in April 1967 and John Charlton in September of that year with special responsibility for the works of Sigmund Freud and other books published in association with the Institute of Psycho-Analysis. Geoffrey Trevelyan continued to take charge of technical and some general books until 1978. On the death of Cecil Day-Lewis, D. J. Enright accepted the invitation to join the board in 1972 as Poetry and Literary Editor. Ian Parsons had been Managing Director since 1954 and brought abundant creative and literary flair to his management of Chatto, in close cooperation with the administrative and artistic skills of Norah Smallwood: their talents were complementary, and when Ian Parsons retired in 1975 Norah Smallwood's task in running the firm was made considerably harder.

Christopher MacLehose joined the board in 1975 after the departure of Ian Parsons, and stayed until November 1979. His editorial contribution to Chatto was the most valuable of the post-war period—he brought the great American writers Toni Morrison and Bernard Malamud to the list, as well as bringing an invigorating modernity and style to Chatto's image.

Hugo Brunner became Joint Managing Director in March 1976, with Norah Smallwood. This period which followed Ian Parsons's retirement was an unsettled time. In February 1977 Hugo Brunner decided to leave to take up an appointment at Oxford University Press. Sebastian Walker, later to become the notable children's book publisher, had been a European sales representative for the Chatto, Bodley Head and Cape group, and joined the Chatto board in September 1977. Within a year he departed and soon set up his own company, Walker Books.

By 1979 Norah Smallwood, now nearing seventy, was suffering from severe arthritis, mainly in her hands, but she would never give in to the pain, and did not wish to retire. In 1979 she invited Hugo Brunner to rejoin the firm, again as Joint Managing Director. One of his colleagues at Oxford University Press, Jeremy Lewis, came to Chatto as a board member at the same time. His was a quintessentially English contribution to the spirit of the Chatto list, and he would remain on the board until 1989. The two years 1980 and 1981 were a kind of interregnum. The end of an era occurred in October 1980 when Ian Parsons died.

It was clear that Chatto needed a new lease of life which was unlikely to begin until Mrs. Smallwood decided to retire. The book trade had been waiting for some time to see what would happen to Chatto in a post-Smallwood era.

There had been many discussions about a possible successor to take over her post as Managing Director of Chatto & Windus. The strongest contender was Carmen Callil, who had founded the Virago Press in 1972. In 1981 the group main board (Graham Greene and Tom Maschler of Cape; Max Reinhardt, Judy Taylor and David Machin of Bodley Head; and Norah Smallwood, Hugo Brunner and John Charlton of Chatto) invited Carmen Callil to join Chatto as Managing Director.

In 1982 Virago was bought by Chatto, Bodley Head and Cape and became the fourth member of the group. The service company for all four firms became known by their initials: CVBC Services, and was based at Bow Street. Virago moved to the top floor of the William IV Street building, with Chatto occupying most of the lower floors.

In March 1982 Norah Smallwood decided to retire and to work at home as a consultant for a further year. Meanwhile Carmen Callil was appointed Joint Managing Director on 10

36

April 1982, forty-five years after Mrs. Smallwood joined Chatto & Windus.

Norah Smallwood died in October 1984, aged seventy-four, in Westminster Hospital. Many tributes were paid to her vibrant, dominant personality, and her services to book publishing, for which she was awarded an OBE in 1973. Her entry in the *Dictionary of National Biography*, written by John Charlton, gives a resumé of her career as a publisher.

Hugo Brunner had become Chairman after the retirement of Norah Smallwood, and he remained on the board until he resigned in May 1985. He had made a considerable contribution to the non-fiction list, with authors such as Richard Cobb, Caroline Davidson, Richard Ingrams and John Piper. He is also remembered for his support of the work of the poet-novelist George Mackay Brown, as well as the publishing of Wilfred Owen and Isaiah Berlin.

The appointment of Carmen Callil resulted in a fresh start for Chatto after a period of a traditional publishing policy. She brought a flair for publicity and saw the importance of lively and contemporary book design, eye-catching jackets and promotional material, and an emphasis on expanding the work of the publicity department.

On her arrival Carmen appointed directors to be in charge of different departments, which was new to Chatto. She was appointed sole Managing Director in March 1983. Barry Featherstone was appointed as Production Director in 1982, and Juliet Nicolson was made Chatto's first ever Publicity Director.

XI

Under Carmen Callil's leadership many new names joined the Chatto fiction list. She promoted established authors as well as those who had not yet made their name, in much the same way as John Camden Hotten had done more than a century before. New authors soon found themselves spurred on by a flurry of encouraging postcards, and many authors who had been with the firm since long before Carmen's time found themselves encountering their greatest success.

With the increasingly large advances paid for well-known authors and the growth of the role of the literary agent in trade publishing, it was important for Chatto to form close relationships with those literary agents who tended to represent the authors that the firm was eager to publish. Among the agencies with whom Chatto has come to do a notable amount of business are Aitken & Stone; Curtis Brown; Elaine Greene; David Higham; A. M. Heath; Deborah Owen; Peters, Fraser & Dunlop; Rogers, Coleridge & White; Tessa Sayle; Abner Stein; Anthony Sheil Associates; Ed Victor and A. P. Watt.

Before Carmen's arrival the design of Chatto's book jackets, though handsome and distinguished, tended to err on the side of modesty. Under her management uniformity of covers and sober front-cover illustrations were dispensed with, to be replaced by bolder designs and full-colour illustrations, frequently occupying the front, spine and back cover of the book. Carmen was tireless in stressing the importance of having an eye-catching design on the spine of a book, as it is often the only part of the volume visible to a customer in a bookshop. As well as the books themselves, 'point-of-sale' material was more carefully designed, and editors learned to write cover blurbs that would avoid Carmen's snort and the epithet 'instant remainder'.

XII

In the 1980s the economic recession hit all publishing companies: high interest rates led to a demand for the reduction of overheads. As a result of cost-cutting measures Bodley Head left Bow Street in 1985 and moved to Bedford Square; in 1986 its production, design and rights departments merged with Cape's. In December 1986 Chatto moved from William IV Street to 30 Bedford Square, the four floors of a Georgian building overlooking the square's plane trees and gardens. Next door at no. 31 were Bodley Head, the group accounts and the Company Secretary, and at no. 30 were Jonathan Cape.

In Carmen Callil's first year as Joint MD the following were members of the Chatto board—in addition to Hugo Brunner and herself—Mike Petty, Editorial Director; Barry Featherstone, Production Director; John Charlton; and Juliet Nicolson, who was replaced, after her departure for America, by Kate Griffin. At the beginning of 1985 Andrew Motion was appointed to the board, later to be Editorial Director, and Christine Carswell, who had previously worked in the Chatto rights department, was appointed Deputy Managing Director; Susanna Porter came from Random House in New York to become Rights Director. Ron Costley, Hilary Laurie, Alison Samuel and Nicole Paulissen were all appointed to the board.

1987 was a momentous year for the Chatto/Virago/ Bodley Head and Cape group, both for changes in the set-up of the group itself and also within Chatto. First Max Reinhardt, Joint Chairman of Bodley Head, resigned to continue to publish his own list from his home. His shares were sold to Tom Maschler and Graham C. Greene of Cape. In May 1987 Graham C. Greene, Group Chairman, announced to the staff that the group had been sold to an American company, Random House.

The years preceding 1987 had been difficult for CVBC. Random House, along with Condé Nast, the magazine publishers, were owned by Si and Bob Newhouse, known to be among the most powerful and dynamic figures in the world of publishing. The takeover seemed to ensure a brighter financial future for the group which had been operating at a loss for some years. Virago decided to buy itself out of the group and become independent once more.

In June 1987 Simon Master, ex-Managing Director of Pan, was appointed Managing Director of Random House UK, replacing Graham C. Greene.

XIII

In June 1989 another momentous event transformed the future of Chatto: in a 'reverse takeover' Random House UK (alias Chatto, Bodley Head and Cape) bought Century Hutchinson. Anthony Cheetham, with his wife Rosemary, Gail Rebuck and Peter Roche, had founded Century ten years previously and had then taken over Hutchinson. He was appointed Chairman and Chief Executive of Random House UK, and Simon Master was appointed Group Managing Director. The name of the group was changed from Random House to Random Century, and a new holding company was formed, on the board of which Carmen Callil, as Managing Director of Chatto, took a seat.

Six months later Anthony Cheetham announced the restructuring of the group into four publishing divisions and a move to a permanent home for all companies to 20 Vauxhall Bridge Road, Pimlico. Chatto & Windus and Cape (which now absorbed Bodley Head) remained separate companies within a division served by a separate sales force. In 1991 Gail Rebuck succeeded Anthony Cheetham as Chairman and Chief Executive of Random Century.

Chatto adapted quickly to its new home on the sixth floor of Random Century House, with its excellent views of London, glimpses of the Thames to the south, the beacon of Canary Wharf to the south-east, the glass dome of the Tate Gallery and the upper part of Parliament's Victoria Tower to the east, and the terracotta tower of Westminster Cathedral to the north. As the *Bookseller* reported in January 1991: 'The Chatto floor has, perhaps, the most distinctive character. Overstuffed, faded easy chairs sit happily with modern office furniture. The entrance is lined with photographs of the division's authors, and bookcases sag under the weight of books. Two canaries called Chatto & Windus occupy a cage outside Carmen Callil's office . . . There is something eccentric, and anarchic, about the Chatto floor.'

Juliet Nicolson, Christine Carswell, Susanna Porter and Catherine Eccles were amongst the most talented young women to enter publishing in the 1980s and each of them made a distinctive and invaluable contribution to Chatto's development, as did the poet Andrew Motion whose period as Editorial Director introduced younger writers and poets—Alan Hollinghurst, Mick Imlah, Peter Conrad, John Fuller—to the Chatto list. He was succeeded by Rupert Lancaster, who came from Cape to join Chatto as Editorial Director in 1988; he brought authors such as Will Carling, Imran Khan and Jason Goodwin to the firm. He was succeeded as Editorial Director in 1990 by Jonathan Burnham who had joined the company in 1987 and whose editorial discretion and inspiration brought renewed strength to Chatto. His editorial team includes the formidable talents of Alison Samuel, Managing Editorial Director of the company since 1985 and Jenny Uglow whose particular responsibility has been to maintain the intellectual standards and traditions of the Hogarth Press. Gail Lynch, who became Publicity Director in 1989, is another member of the young and energetic group of directors recruited by Carmen, all of

41

whom were under thirty years old. Their comparative youth was balanced by the experience of other directors on the Chatto board including John Charlton, now Chairman of the company, who has been with Chatto since 1965; Carmen herself; and Barry Featherstone, Production Director, who has been a cornerstone of Chatto since 1967.

XIV

Throughout the various changes in personnel at Chatto & Windus over the last few years, the firm has managed to maintain a name, not only for the consistently high quality of the books it has published, but also for the enterprising way that these books have been presented to the public.

If one considers the achievements of four prominent authors who have been with the firm for over twenty-five years, Chatto's claim to be publishers of works of enduring literary quality seems wholly justified.

Chatto has published all Iris Murdoch's twenty-four novels since her debut with *Under the Net* in 1954. She won the Booker Prize for *The Sea, The Sea* in 1978. In addition to her celebrated novels she has also published four books of philosophy—she has been a Fellow at St. Anne's College, Oxford since 1948 and has taught the subject there—as well as poetry and plays. She was appointed a DBE in 1987.

A. S. Byatt's first novel, *Shadow of a Sun*, came out in 1964, and since then Chatto has published four more novels and a short-story collection. She won the Booker Prize in 1990 for her most recent novel, *Possession*. She is also well known as a literary critic, and has worked tirelessly for the cause of literature, as a university lecturer and as a broadcaster, and as Chairman of the Society of Authors. She was appointed a CBE in 1990.

Chatto has been publishing the books of V. S. Pritchett since 1935. His ten collections of stories—Paul Theroux has called him 'our best short-story writer'—were gathered together in one volume in 1990, the year of his ninetieth birthday, and Chatto published his essays on literature in another single-volume collection in 1991. His work also includes three volumes of biography, on Balzac, Turgenev and Chekhov; five novels; seven travel books, and two volumes of autobiography: *A Cab at the Door* and *Midnight Oil*. V. S. Pritchett has been President of the Society of Authors for many years, President of International PEN and he was knighted in 1975.

Laurens van der Post, who was born in Africa in 1906, came to live in England in the 1930s. His first novel, *In a Province*, was published in 1934 by the Hogarth Press, and his many books since then, with their powerful narratives and wide imaginative range, in particular his stories of exploration in Africa, include *Venture to the Interior* (1952), and notably, *The Lost World of the Kalahari* (1958). Soldier, explorer, close friend of Jung, his later autobiographical books—*Yet Being Someone Other* (1982), *A Walk With a White Bushman* (1986) and *About Blady* (1991)—have confirmed him as a man of exceptional vision. He was awarded a CBE in 1947 for gallant and distinguished services in the field, and was knighted in 1981.

As well as the authors discussed above, other well-known novelists whose work has been on the Chatto list for many years and is still available are: Aldous Huxley, Raymond Williams, Mary Hocking, Dirk Bogarde, Lynne Reid Banks, the Nobel Prize winner William Faulkner, along with other outstanding American writers.

Toni Morrison is best known for her novel *Beloved*, for which she won the Pulitzer Prize in 1989; the sequel to this, *Jazz*, will be published in 1992. Among other books, Anne Tyler is the author of *The Accidental Tourist* (1985) and *Saint Maybe*, which was published in 1991. David

Malouf, Australia's most eminent poet and novelist, is the author of *An Imaginary Life* (1978), a remarkable recreation of the exile of the Roman poet, Ovid. He was the recipient of the prestigious Pascall prize in 1988, and his most recent novel, *The Great World*, was received with rapture in 1990, and won the 1991 Commonwealth Writers Prize. He has also written volumes of autobiography and poetry.

The loyalty to Chatto of those authors with an established reputation has helped to keep the firm in a position of high standing. Many major prizes and awards have been won in recent years: as well as the Booker Prize winners, Dame Iris Murdoch in 1978 and A. S. Byatt in 1990, Booker Prize short-lists have included Timothy Mo's *An Insular Possession* and *The Redundancy of Courage*, Iris Murdoch's *The Book and The Brotherhood*, Marina Warner's *The Lost Father*, and Mordecai Richler's *Solomon Gursky Was Here*. The Commonwealth Writers Prize has been a demonstration of the catholicity of the Chatto list. Mordecai Richler was the outright winner in 1990, and David Malouf in 1991. Marina Warner was short-listed in 1989, Paul Griffiths in 1990, and A. S. Byatt, David Malouf and Alice Munro in 1991. A. S. Byatt also won the *Irish Times*/Aer Lingus International Fiction Prize in 1990 for *Possession*, and Marina Warner a Macmillan Silver Pen Award for *The Lost Father* in 1989. Margaret Forster won the prestigious Royal Society of Literature Award in 1988 for her biography of Elizabeth Barrett Browning. In 1990 the W. H. Smith Annual Literary Award went to V. S. Pritchett for his short-story collection, *A Careless Widow*.

Many important novelists joined Chatto in the last ten years, since Carmen Callil took the helm. Angela Carter's relationship with Chatto began in 1984 with *Nights at the Circus*, though her relationship with Carmen Callil (through Virago) goes back to her early career. Acclaimed for her shorter fiction, and for her acute and uncompromising non-fiction, she is above all known as a stunningly imaginative

44

and inventive novelist. Her most recent novel, *Wise Children*, was published to universal acclaim in June 1991. Since publishing her first novel in 1965, Margaret Forster has become a popular and highly regarded author of fiction. Chatto has published her work since 1986, and her books include *Have The Men Had Enough?* and *The Battle for Christabel*. John Fuller has come to be regarded as one of the most prodigiously varied and technically accomplished poets writing in Britain; Chatto have published his two most recent collections. He is also a celebrated novelist, and Chatto has published three of his novels. Chatto published Timothy Mo's third novel, *An Insular Possession*, in 1986. Great critical attention greeted the publication of *The Redundancy of Courage*, a magnificent tale of warfare and betrayal, in April 1991. Marina Warner, the author of important books on art history and cultural criticism, wrote her first novel, *The Lost Father*, in 1988, which was followed by *Indigo*, to be published by Chatto in 1991. The first novel by Alan Hollinghurst, *The Swimming-Pool Library*, was among the most acclaimed first novels published in Britain since the war and Josephine Hart's extraordinary first novel *Damage*, published in 1991, became an international best-seller. Tim O'Grady, Glenn Patterson, Paul Griffiths, Polly Devlin and Tariq Ali were among the many first novelists published by Chatto in the 1980s, and younger British novelists showed formidable promise: Sara Maitland, Patrick Gale, D. J. Taylor and Rose Boyt.

Many important novelists from across the Atlantic joined the Chatto list in the 1980s: two Canadians, the short-story writer Alice Munro, and the comic genius Mordecai Richler. From the United States came the author of *Dispatches*, Michael Herr, with a highly original novel, *Walter Winchell*; the ebullient Erica Jong; the distinguished novelist and biographer, Diane Johnson, and the spell-binding story teller, Anne Rice. Many younger American writers have also joined the list: Emily Prager, Bobbie Ann Mason, Seth

Morgan, Susanna Moore, with Whitgift, Mary Gaitskill and Richard Russo, each with a new and individual American voice.

Many Australian authors joined Chatto too: the cartoonist Victoria Roberts whose work now adorns the covers and pages of the *New Yorker*, C. J. Koch, Lee Tulloch, Tom Shapcott and Tom Keneally, writing popular fiction under the pseudonym William Coyle.

Popular story-telling has always been a Chatto tradition and Celia Brayfield had two considerable successes with Chatto, *Pearls* and *The Prince*. Ann Victoria Roberts is among the most talented writers to join Chatto and her duet of novels, *Louisa Elliott* and *Liam's Story*, were classics of the story-telling art.

Chatto also began to publish crime writers in the 1990s, and Liza Cody and her splendid female sleuth, Anna Lee, joined the list with Dorothy Dunnett, creator of the gentleman detective, Johnson Johnson.

Chatto has always been the proud publisher of translations of the works of distinguished foreign writers. Before the war these included Luigi Pirandello, Proust, Chekhov, Gogol, Strindberg and others. In the 1960s the list included Ercole Patti, Michele Pantaleone, Par Lagerkvist, Jiri Mucha, Alexandre Benois and Alexander Herzen. Today there are Joseph Roth, Antonio Tabucchi, Libuse Monikova, Gregor von Rezzori and Bohumil Hrabal. Chatto continues to publish the works of Israel's finest writer, Amos Oz, and has recently added four novels by Ivan Klíma that were banned in his native Czechoslovakia, including the masterpiece, *Judge on Trial*, in 1991. Chatto also publishes the work of Christoph Ransmayr as well as six novels and the autobiography of the Russian Nina Berberova.

Chatto's renowned translation (by C. K. Scott Moncrieff) of Proust's *A La Recherche du Temps Perdu*, based on the Pléiade edition from Gallimard, was superseded in 1981 by a new three-volume edition of *Remembrance of Things Past*, which was based on the Scott Moncrieff translation but extensively revised by Terence Kilmartin according to a new French edition of 1954. Proust completed an alternative version of *Albertine Disparue*, the seventh volume of *A La Recherche du Temps Perdu*. This version—a hand-corrected typescript—was rediscovered after the death of Proust's niece in 1986. Terence Kilmartin translated this and Chatto published it in 1989.

Terence Kilmartin died in August 1991, as he was approaching completion of a new edition of Proust to incorporate all the new material that became available on the publication in France of the new Pléiade edition. D. J. Enright was able to complete the work on this revised edition, due to appear under the new title of *In Search of Lost Time*.

XV

Besides the injection of new life into Chatto's fiction list, the 1980s saw Chatto acquire a prestigious number of writers of non-fiction, especially in the field of biography and contemporary journalism, and criticism. The most notable amongst these new arrivals are Michael Holroyd, Edmund White—whose fiction will also be published by Chatto—Brian Masters, William Shawcross, Christopher Hitchens, Francis Wheen, Malise Ruthven, Nick Humphrey, Peter Fuller, Edward W. Said, R. W. Johnson, Francis Wyndham, Lucretia Stewart, Peter Conrad and Michael Ignatieff. The two latter writers demonstrate the versatility of the younger generation of authors on the Chatto list inasmuch as Peter Conrad, most noted as a critic and cultural historian, publishes his first novel in 1992, and Michael Ignatieff, writer of philosophy and autobiography, made a remarkable debut as a novelist with *Asya* in 1991. The journalists Valerie

47

Grove, Mavis Nicholson and Suzanne Lowry also published with Chatto from the 1980s onwards.

True to its tradition, Chatto has published many outstanding biographies and autobiographies in the last ten years. The major biography in this period was *Bernard Shaw* by Michael Holroyd. 'When the three great volumes are complete they will take their place among the great biographies,' declared William Golding in 1989. The three volumes are all now published, with a fourth and final volume to come, containing notes and an epilogue by Holroyd on Shaw.

Other literary biographies include: the reissue in one volume of George Painter's classic study of Proust; a two-volume definitive life of Vladimir Nabokov by Brian Boyd; Lyndall Hopkinson's portrait of her mother, Antonia White; *Sylvia Plath* by L. Wagner Martin; Brian Masters's entertaining life of E. F. Benson; biographies of Ngaio Marsh, Compton Mackenzie, Jean Stafford, Josephine Baker, and a highly acclaimed life of Elizabeth Barrett Browning by Margaret Forster. Nicholas Wapshott has written excellent biographies of Carol Reed and Rex Harrison. Awards have been made for such exemplary biographies as *Sylvia Townsend Warner* by Clare Harman (the *Mail on Sunday*/John Llewellyn Rhys Prize, 1989) and *Tom Driberg: His Life and Indiscretions* by Francis Wheen, which won the 1991 Somerset Maugham Award.

Many autobiographers have put pen to paper for Chatto since this book first appeared; among them Angelica Garnett and Brian Inglis, as well as two volumes each from Michael Wharton, N. K. Chaudhuri and Elspeth Huxley, and three volumes from Richard Hoggart and Ralph Glasser. Hoggart's seminal book, *The Uses of Literacy*, was also published by Chatto. Best-selling memoirs from famous actors are Dirk Bogarde's three volumes, Kenneth Branagh's *Beginning* and Antony Sher's *Year of the King*; and celebrities from the world of sport, Imran Khan and Will Carling, have also contributed reminiscences.

XVI

Chatto maintains a distinguished poetry list. Following in the tradition of Ian Parsons, Cecil Day-Lewis and D. J. Enright, Andrew Motion and Mick Imlah have both brought new talent to the list. Ian Parsons published the poems of Edmund Blunden, Isaac Rosenberg, Wilfred Owen, William Plomer, William Empson and George Mackay Brown. Cecil Day-Lewis in particular fostered the Phoenix Living Poets series which included many distinguished names: Patric Dickinson, D. J. Enright, John Fuller, P. J. Kavanagh, Anne Sexton, Jon Stallworthy and Scotland's greatest living poet, Norman MacCaig—and continued the Chatto tradition which lasts to this day of publishing translations: the poems of Cavafy and Rilke, for example. When Cecil Day-Lewis died in May 1972 the poet D. J. Enright (later to be awarded the Queen's Medal for Poetry and an OBE) was appointed Poetry Editor. During this period Chatto published poems of Elizabeth Bishop, Nobel Prize-winner Eugenio Montale, Theodore Weiss, Sylvia Townsend Warner, John Hartley Williams—and D. J. Enright's own poetry collections.

In 1985 Andrew Motion, another distinguished poet, was appointed Poetry Editor, and the Phoenix series was gradually replaced by a new-format poetry series of living poets. Andrew Motion published first collections from Selima Hill, Carol Rumens, Fred d'Aguiar and Alan Jenkins, to name a few.

When Andrew Motion left the firm, Mick Imlah, a Chatto poet and former editor of *Poetry Review*, was appointed in his place. Chatto continues to publish the poetry of John Fuller and the work of Norman MacCaig. The list continues to flourish with poets such as Robert Crawford, Gerard Woodward, Peter Reading, Mark Ford, Lachlan Mackinnon and Bernard O'Donoghue.

Chatto has also published several anthologies, among them John Fuller's *The Chatto Book of Love Poetry* and Francis Spufford's eclectic collection of lists, *The Chatto Book of Cabbages and Kings*.

XVII

Under Carmen Callil's direction Chatto's range of illustrated books has grown to embrace much of the natural world. The celebrated studies of the flowers of Greece and the Mediterranean by Anthony Huxley (with co-authors William Taylor and Oleg Polunin) have been followed up by lavish horticultural books such as *The Englishwoman's Garden, The New Englishwoman's Garden, Brilliant Gardens* and *Rose Gardens* by Jane Fearnley-Whittingstall, and *The Flowering Year* by Anna Pavord.

Beleaguered and misunderstood animals found protection under Carmen's wing. Les and Sue Stocker, owners of the remarkable St. Tiggywinkle's Wildlife Hospital, wrote *The Complete Hedgehog* and persuaded a generation to love these small and spiny nocturnal mammals. Otters, bats, owls and garden birds have all had their chance to appear in print, and aristocratic felines allowed the world a glimpse into their boudoirs in *The English Cat at Home*.

The Chatto kitchen has also become renowned for gastronomic enterprise. Both Lynda Brown and Frances Bissell, before she became *The Times* cookery correspondent, wrote their first cookbooks for Chatto. The well-known broadcaster Mollie Harris engineered a bibulous evening bout in the Chatto offices on the publication of *A Drop O' Wine*. M. F. K. Fisher travelled great distances, and her humorous and elegant writings on food opened up an entirely new way of appreciating the shorter journey from plate to mouth. The great Claudia Roden and Thane Prince, the *Telegraph* cookery correspondent, have both come up with very successful titles for Chatto.

Many books on art and architecture and interior design have found their place on the Chatto list: Christopher Sykes's *Private Palaces* and *Ancient English Houses* were joined by Lucinda Lambton's *An Album of Curious Houses*. *The Englishwoman's Bedroom, Biedermeier* and *The House and Garden Book of Classic Rooms* were accompanied by *The World of Mary Ellen Best*, a fine-art book of early nineteenth-century interiors.

Other fine-art books include: *Jacques-Louis David* by Anita Brookner; *Piper's Places* by John Piper and Richard Ingrams; *State of the Art* by Sandy Nairne; *Theoria: Art and the Absence of Grace* by Peter Fuller; Eric Shanes's two books on Turner; *Romanesque Art* by Meyer Schapiro; a paperback series on Illuminated Manuscripts of the Middle Ages; an illustrated paperback, *How to Look at Modern Art* by Philip Yenawine, Director of Education at the Museum of Modern Art, New York. Recent biographies furnished with handsome illustrations are *Queen Victoria* by E. F. Benson and *Ford Madox Brown* by Teresa Newman and Ray Watkinson.

Books of photographs continue to appear. The Hogarth Press published *Victorian Photographs of Famous Men and Fair Women* by Julia Margaret Cameron, revised and reissued in 1973. Two collections of the photographs of Jane Bown became one volume, *Portraits*, in 1990. Chatto also published *The Treasures of Eton*, Rosamond Lehmann's *Album, Friends in Focus* by Frances Partridge, and Janet Stone's *Thinking Faces*.

In 1988, while Rupert Lancaster was a director of Chatto, he was made responsible for the publicity and distribution of Fodor's Travel Guides. The Fodor list is now administered by Rupert Lancaster as a separate company within the Random Century group.

Apart from Chatto's association with Fodor's Guides, travel books have always formed an important part of the Chatto list. Vikram Seth's *From Heaven Lake* won the Thomas Cook Travel Award in 1983. Stevenson's *Travels with a Donkey in the Cevennes* and Hakluyt's *Voyages* were reissued. Bettina Selby wrote two entertaining books on the joys of pedal power; Annette Kobak's life of Isabelle Eberhardt, Imran Khan's *Indus Journey*, Radek Sikorski's remarkable account of his journey through war-torn Afghanistan, and Jason Goodwin's history of the tea trade, *The Gunpowder Gardens*, continued that tradition.

XVIII

In the 1930s the Hogarth Press published a series called The Hogarth Letters: single essays by writers such as Rebecca West, H. G. Wells, E. M. Forster and Virginia Woolf, reissued in one volume in 1985. In May 1989 the art of the pamphlet was revived with Chatto CounterBlasts. Pamphlets to date have included writers as various as A. N. Wilson, Sue Townsend, Ludovic Kennedy, William Shawcross and Brenda Maddox on subjects as diverse as religion, the welfare state, euthanasia, Hong Kong and abortion.

Carmen Callil commissioned this series of slim paperbacks: 'It is a return to the eighteenth-century idea of the publisher as disseminator of ideas. Too many people feel that nothing can be done about things. I wanted to stir the pot, and encourage people to object and argue, and feel that writers can bring about change.' Longer pamphlets on more international themes were written by Ralf Dahrendorf and Shirley Hazzard.

And Chatto has always kept alive the tradition of polemical literature. In recent years it has published, for example: *Error of Judgement: The Truth about the Birmingham Bombings* by Labour MP, Chris Mullin; *White Lies*, the story of a modern-day lynching by Nick Davies; *The Shah's Last Ride* by William Shawcross; *A Satanic Affair: Salman Rushdie and the Rage of Islam* by Malise Ruthven; *Blood, Class and Nostalgia* by Christopher Hitchens, a study of 'Anglophilia, Anglophobia, Anglo-Americanism and Anglo-Saxondom'. In 1990 Chatto published *The Beauty Myth* by a Rhodes scholar, Naomi Wolf, an exposé of the age-old cult of female beauty. *The Chatto Book of Dissent*, edited by Michael Rosen and David Widgery, was published in 1991.

British and foreign histories have always been part of Chatto's publishing projects. In recent years there have been some stimulating and scholarly books. Recent books on Europe have included: *Operation Autonomous* by Ivor Porter, who was parachuted into Roumania in 1943; *The Making of Eastern Europe* by Z. A. B. Zeman, published in February 1989 before the momentous changes occurred but offering penetrating and controversial arguments about the discontinuities between Eastern and Western Europe; Gerd Ruge's informative biography of Gorbachev, published by Chatto in 1991; memoirs of Germany in the Second World War by Marie 'Missie' Vassiltchikov and Christabel Bielenberg; Svetlana Alexievich's *Zinky Boys*, interviews with Russians abut the war in Afghanistan; William Shawcross's *Dubcek and Czechoslovakia* was reissued by the Hogarth Press at a timely moment, as was his authoritative account of the war in Cambodia, *Sideshow*.

Malise Ruthven's *The Divine Supermarket* examines the religious spirit of America. A leading authority on the history and culture of China, Professor John King Fairbank, wrote *The Great Chinese Revolution 1800–1985*; and in 1988 Chatto brought out a moving chronicle by the Oscar-winning star of the film, *The Killing Fields*, Dr. Haing Ngor.

The recent history of Israel has been chronicled by Israel's leading writer, Amos Oz, in various books translated for Chatto. Chatto's range has also extended to fine archaeological/historical studies: Iain Browning's definitive studies of Petra, Palmyra and Jerash, *Baalbek* by Friedrich Ragette and *Jerusalem* by Martin Gilbert. The books published by Professor Sir Moses Finley have become standard works— titles such as *The Ancient Greeks, The World of Odysseus, The Use and Abuse of History* and *The Ancient Economy*. Another classic work, still being reprinted by Chatto, is Gibbon's *Decline and Fall of the Roman Empire*, edited and abridged in one volume by D. M. Low.

On a lighter note, Chatto has published five 'how-to' books on surviving modern life by the columnist Laurie Graham. The Hogarth Press has re-issued in paperback many of the hilarious novels of E. F. Benson. In 1984 the humorous drawings of Roger Pettiward—'Paul Crum'— were collected into a volume entitled *The Last Cream Bun*. He was, alas, killed leading his commando troops in Dieppe in 1942: his death was a grievous loss to British art. In 1985 Chatto produced in one large-format volume a selection from the magazine *Night and Day* which was published by the firm as a weekly magazine in the late 1930s and gives a vivid picture of the style and brilliance of London at that time. Chatto recently published two omnibi of Armistead Maupin's 'Tales of the City', his incomparable vision of gay and bohemian life in San Francisco in the 1980s.

One Chatto book provoked unexpected humour: in 1976 Chatto brought out *The World of Alphonse Allais*, selected, translated and introduced by Miles Kington. Allais has been described as the greatest humorous writer France ever produced. Its publication had a dire effect on one reader, who wrote a letter of complaint that not only was it 'the worst example of typesetting I can remember from a reputable publisher' but that, although he found the offending volume highly entertaining, the book had spontaneously combusted on his bookshelf at home during the night, damaging the two adjacent books from which steam was rising. D. J. Enright, a Chatto director at that time, was asked to write to the gentleman, and he set out some of the details that had beset the publication of this volume: 'the laminators reported that the jackets refused to accept lamination . . . The printer sent the sheets to the wrong binder, where they lay unnoticed for some considerable time. Eventually the sheets were forwarded to the right binders, but alas the right binder's binding machine had now gone wrong. Later, advance copies of the book, printed, bound and laminated against great odds, were put on the wrong train, or possibly on the wrong part of the right train, and consigned to a siding.'

Perhaps if Ruari Maclean had seen the above book before writing *Modern Book Design* his praise of Chatto & Windus as having 'probably the longest unbroken record of excellence in book design' would have been more muted, but by and large it still holds true.

Chatto has always published drama and continues to do so now, and many of its novels and books of other genres have been adapted for film and TV. In the late 1970s four books of plays by Alan Ayckbourn were published. In 1981 the Hogarth Press published *Virginia*, a play by Edna O'Brien—and it was performed at the Theatre Royal Haymarket with Maggie Smith as Virginia Woolf. *Freshwater*, by Virginia Woolf, was published in 1976 and is a spoof on the author's great aunt, Julia Cameron, the Victorian photographer. Chatto's new paperback series of playscripts for publication in 1991 include a translation of Racine's *Bajazet* by Alan Hollinghurst and *The Jewel Box*, the libretto of a new Mozart opera assembled by Paul Griffiths. *Aspects of Love* by David Garnett was adapted as a West End musical, as was Daisy Ashford's enduring tale, *The Young Visiters*.

More modern media have not been ignored. Many of

Iris Murdoch's novels have been adapted and broadcast on television and radio, as has Virginia Woolf's *To the Lighthouse*. Laurens van der Post has made several films based on his experiences of Africa, as well as a three-part television series on the life of Carl Gustav Jung. Chatto published the novels of Maggie Brooks, and her *Loose Connections* was made into a film. In 1991 Chatto published Peter Greenaway's book, *Prospero's Books*, the screenplay of his adaptation for film of Shakespeare's *The Tempest*. Several films are under consideration in 1991: the Russian film industry is to co-operate on a cinematic production of Virginia Woolf's quasi-autobiographical novel, *Orlando*. *A Room of One's Own* was adapted for the stage, with Eileen Atkins as Virginia Woolf. An American film company intends to adapt A. S. Byatt's brilliant novel, *Possession*, for the cinema and Louis Malle is filming Josephine Hart's novel, *Damage*. Josephine Hart was responsible for the adaptation of Iris Murdoch's *The Black Prince* at the Aldwych Theatre.

XIX

The Hogarth Press continues to publish the works of its founders, Virginia and Leonard Woolf. *A Passionate Apprentice: The Early Journals 1897–1909*, by Virginia Woolf, edited by Mitchell Leaska, were until 1990 the only writings never to have appeared in print. Her five volumes of diaries have now appeared in a one-volume abridgement, *A Moment's Liberty: The Shorter Diary*, edited by Anne Olivier Bell, and Hogarth published the abridgement of her six volumes of letters *Congenial Spirits: The Selected Letters of Virginia Woolf*, edited and introduced by Susan Dick. Three hardback volumes of *The Essays of Virginia Woolf*—the first complete edition of Virginia Woolf's non-fiction pieces—have recently appeared, edited by Andrew McNeillie. In 1990 the Hogarth Press reissued her nine novels in a limited numbered hardback edition and in 1991, the fiftieth anniversary of Virginia Woolf's death, this collected edition was made available to a wider public—each novel can now be bought individually. A revised edition of Quentin Bell's biography, *Virginia Woolf*, was published in July 1990.

In 1984, with the rapid rise of paperback publishing, Carmen Callil decided to launch a Hogarth Press Paperbacks list, reissuing some backlist titles from the Hogarth hardback list, as well as out-of-print titles from other publishers. The distinctive purple cover design gave elegance and style to a modern eclectic list which included fiction, biography and poetry. Some eyebrows were raised at the departure from the style that characterised the publications of the Woolfs.

In 1990 Hogarth introduced new hardbacks under the general editorship of Jenny Uglow. These hardback editions provided a forum for writers who combine scholarship with provocative ideas in a new royal format with attractively designed jackets on a black background with the wolf colophon on the spine. Among the authors published are John Lucas, David Kalstone, Peter Raby and Gillian Tindall; appropriately too there is an anthology of Freud's writings on women edited by Elisabeth Young-Bruehl, and *Isaiah Berlin: A Celebration*, a collection of essays to honour Sir Isaiah's eightieth birthday. At the same time reissues of the Hogarth/Chatto backlist continue to be published in paperback by Hogarth in a larger elegant format with a black spine and original cover designs by the brilliant Australian artist, Jeff Fisher: books by Peter Fuller, William Empson, William Shawcross, Michael Ignatieff and many others. Charles Rycroft's celebrated writings on dreams and psycho-analysis were reissued to coincide with the publication of his new book, *Viewpoints*. Hogarth also continues to publish the twenty-four-volume *Standard Edition of the Complete Psychological Works of Sigmund Freud*, translated and edited by James Strachey.

XX

Modern printing technology has revolutionised book production methods in the last decade. No longer is type set laboriously by hand in hot metal, for the typesetter now has a computer-controlled scanner with which to typeset a book. Costs of typesetting have decreased and speed has increased, but the cost of corrections remains high. At the printer—which now contains an in-house bindery—modern machinery such as the Web offset printer has increased the speed of printing, as has the use of jacket folding machines which can perform all operations previously done by hand, including the wrapping of jackets on the books. So jacket printers can now deliver jackets direct to book printers, and books which previously took three or four weeks to produce can now be printed, bound, jacketed and packed under one roof. The quality of printing remains high, but the cost of using top quality paper has also risen. To reduce costs paper is now bought in bulk on a group basis, and paper used is part mechanical (i.e. wood pulp plus chemical constituents) which gives a good result and also saves trees.

In the last decade three firms in particular have given great support to Chatto/Hogarth: the printers, Mackays of Chatham (with whom Random Century have a close business agreement); the printers Butler and Tanner of Frome, Somerset, and Rowland Phototypesetting of Bury St. Edmunds. These firms are renowned for their quality of work and their reliability in meeting often difficult schedules. To give examples of 'problem' assignments: Mackays dealt swiftly in reprinting *Possession* by A. S. Byatt: they printed 20,000 copies in four days even though each copy of the book had washed tops and ribbon markers; Butler and Tanner printed 25,000 copies of *Orchestra!* by Jan Younghusband (a Channel Four TV tie-in) in five days, using five printing machines simultaneously; and Rowland's, as usual, did not blench when confronted with the difficult setting of all kinds of verse (and line drawings) in *The Chatto Book of Nonsense Poetry* (edited by Hugh Haughton). And to name but one jacket printer, White Quill Press of Mitcham have given a consistently high quality of printing and speed of service in producing jackets for Chatto/Hogarth.

While Chatto was still at William IV Street an agreement was made in 1985 with the University of Reading that University library should house the Chatto archives—not only correspondence and stockbooks and other records from the past but the archives of the future. Michael Bott was appointed Keeper of Archives and Manuscripts from October 1985 and remains in charge of this important store of transactions and papers which scholars can inspect and use. Formerly scholars had to visit the Chatto offices for their research but now their requests should be sent direct to Michael Bott who will oversee their visits to the archive. The Chatto File Library of books is housed at one of the group's warehouses in Tiptree, Essex. The other group warehouse, at Grantham in Lincolnshire, has been responsible for storing and distributing all Chatto/Hogarth books since it was opened in 1975.

The Chatto sales force is active throughout the United Kingdom and Europe, and has representatives throughout the Commonwealth where Chatto books are sold. In the United Kingdom the sales force's work is greatly assisted by the development in recent years of tele-ordering by bookshops and EPOS (Electronic Point of Sale) stock control systems. Orders can now be transmitted electronically, with consequent savings in delivery times. The in-house computer system now allows sales departments to gain access to up-to-the-minute information on any account or title.

XXI

Chatto's role in the 1990s will doubtless be influenced by considerations affecting the publishing industry as a whole—the increasing tendency towards international links, the changing patterns of book-selling in general and the Net Book Agreement in particular, and the whole question of how books should be published, whether in hardback or in paperback or in some other form. Chatto & Windus and the Hogarth Press, as the active imprints for a truly exceptional list of authors, and as an intact vigorous publishing force within the Random Century group, will doubtless be helping to determine these questions in a positive and distinctive way. As this book goes to press 1992 is about to begin, with the threatened demise of the Net Book Agreement and the possible end of one of the worst recessions the book trade has ever known. What remains paramount to a publishing company with a list of high quality such as that of Chatto & Windus is the successful publishing, selling and satisfaction of its authors: the future of the company, as Chatto & Windus nears the end of a century and a half as book publishers, lies with them and the people at Chatto who work for them.